Diary of Rhymes

ALSO BY JEMELIA MOSELEY

Love, Joy, Tears, Beers and Poetry

DIARY

OF

RHYMES

Jemelia Moseley

QUERENCIA

QUERENCIA PRESS

© Copyright 2023
Jemelia Moseley

ISBN 978 1 959118 47 3

www.querenciapress.com

First Published in 2023

Querencia Press, LLC
Chicago IL

Printed & Bound in the United States of America

CONTENTS

for my children, I love you forever and always, may you always be blessed

SUNDAY VIBES

Sunday music, aka reggae, blasting through the stereo
in between the DJ's annoying 'rewind come again selector' inputs.
The scent of incense trying to mask the smell of Rice and Peas and a choice of a poor animal
that didn't make it—probably a Goat or Chicken.

Weekly visits to Grandma and Grandad's house, followed by the cleaning.
Their house full—like my belly, bursting at the seams.

Grandma's house shakes from all our games and our screams.
We argue about who got more Guinness Punch or carrot juice, we play
Murder in the Dark, we play and we lark.

The Heartbeat and Upper Hand theme tune—the sign of night drawing nigh.
I watch the stars floating high
As we drive through the dark streets of Tottenham and Wood Green.

I stare at the dark through the window,
counting stars, as my eyes burn from the tiredness that lurks.
I fight mentally to keep them open, but I find I'm upon my bed in pyjamas unaware of how I
got there.

I whisper my prayers
and ask God to protect me and those I love;
I also pray for the strangers that I do not know.

MY DESTINY

Through choppy waters, tranquil by day, beautiful by sight, unkind at a touch
on a shady dingy.
Risking life and limb to attempt to arrive safely to shore, safely onto secure land
because the man in suits told the man in arms to invade my motherland.

We're poisoned by the gas and by the slaughter of our people.

Destruction, devastation, and death.

The only thing left is the touch of my dying mother's shaking hand,
her tears fall like my people.

Like her hope, their spirits rise.

I set ashore
to death or to float
to sink or to swim
to drown or to live
my destiny, to die or to be free.

I WILL WEAR MY CROWN

In my loneliest days
In my darkest hour
dents in my structure will not hold me down
I will get up, dust myself off
and wear my crown

In the eeriness of the unknown
surrounded by the familiar smell of the ones I hold close to me
in the depths of my insecurity
of what comes before and after me
I will wear my crown

When my days are unkind
and my nights are worse
I will think about all I have overcome
and all that I have become
and all that is yet to come
and until my days are done
I will wear my crown

BURIED

And just like that...
the church songs were sung by one, ensured by Covid and speeches where we attempted to right
our hurtful wrongs.

We sum you up in paragraphs
in paraphrases, with more tears, and with some laughs.

We gather at the graveside, carefully avoiding your new neighbours as they gather close, too
close for comfort.

We sing hymns as we hold each other by our weak limbs.

Life will never be the same.
We pray and we chant your name,
as we place you upon your beloved.
Knowing that when we leave and the night sets in, the lucky little insects, they may creep in—
upon your body they lay, thieving my hug, covering you the way I wish I still could.
Feasting upon your, like I loved to feast at your mind.

One of a kind.
To walk away now, knowing that there's no going back—
only to lay you flowers that will placed upon a stone.
No more cards, no more chocolates, no more speaking to you on the phone.

Just flowers,

upon your grave

where we stand//pretending we are brave//when really we want to cave in—

like your body now but not your soul—

decaying

ravished//by grief and the shame of not giving you more.

Heart shattered into pieces, scars forever sore,

and these scars will bleed for the lifetime that I will now spend without you.

I REPRESENT THE COLOURS OF THE RAINBOW

—written for LGBT week

I am Queer
I stand tall with love, without fear.

I represent the colours of the rainbow,
I will shine bright through the sun and the rain.
I am looking for the gold
I lose, I love, and I gain.

My heart is pure, and my love is free,
yet some judge.
They judge
who I am
what I am
who I love.
Even though they claim love is love.

Some say I cannot seek blessings from above
as such my feeling can be repressed and impaled.
Years later we've improved, but I'm not impressed,
we've still failed.
We're still on a journey to be free, to be equal, to excel.

I am queer
I have rights
we are a part of the future
see the light
be the light.

IN MY SCHOOL

In my school there were rules,
to prepare you for the real world.

The real world, governed by men—maybe a woman or two.
The real graft
Less laughs
Less warm hearts
Less friends
Wrong turns lead to dead ends.

Promises get broken by lovers and friends.
The meaning of family means more than it did then.
The knowledge and wisdom I have now I didn't have then.
The rules of the world, I now understand them.

How I have that feeling of wishing we could start again,
in my school full of rules.

FROM CARE

They ask why I care so deeply
How would you feel if you were
left or taken, then
abandoned at 18.

Left to fend for oneself.
On birthdays, Christmas, or other celebrations
no family to make a fuss.
Like the last one left on the shelf,
they await their home
where they will belong
where they deserve to be.

My heart yearns to give—

home cooked meals,
shopping for more than one,
love that cannot be undone.
Continuity to tuck you in at night,
security that care cannot buy.
Consistency that care cannot provide.
A life story you, not a Social Worker, will write.

I AM MORE THAN MY HAIR

As a black child growing up in the 90's, they said I was lucky because my hair was long,
when I cut it, they said my beauty was gone.
They said my 'bird legs' needed meat,
when on holiday, they said the sun would turn my lips black, I should protect them from the
heat.

Flamingo was my name.
Skinny with striking long hair,
it's all they saw, not the rise to my fall or all them closed doors and them closing in walls.

Some long days and summer nights,
I stayed awake preparing to fight.
Throwing away all my fears and getting rid of the never-ending fright.

Through my ambitions and losing my inhibitions,
I made my life alright.
Do not judge me, you do not know what I have been through as I stand before you in this light.

I am more than my hair.
In my shoes, I have stumbled and walked.
With my mouth, I prayed and I talked.

I have visions of my missions and I know he listens.
As I aim to accomplish my dreams, I dream of a life of freedom.
Where my pain will be eased and my family and friends will know peace.
Where I will mean more than my skin colour
and where I will mean more than my hair.

MISERY LOVES COMPANY

I am watching TV as the TV watches me.
I see movement but I hear no sound.
In my own head space, my own maze,
feeling really lost and I really want to be found.

The comfort of misery keeps misery surrounding me,
yet I am so very lonely.

I pray for strength, that my ancestors guide me.
My history seems to define me.
The unspoken, the untold
the truth and the hidden
the secrets and the unforbidden.
All the things I did
and didn't
get to love and to hold.
Holding on to the things you love, that you outgrow.
Holding onto things that get old.
And it's true what they say...peace of mind and love can never be bought or sold

YOU

As I kneel from where I stand
I place my world, my whole life in your hands.

Hopes, dreams, and wishes.
My fears, wins, and all my misses.

When I'm surrounded,
when I'm alone,
I feel you in my heart, like the spirits that shine down like the stars.
They watch over me.
They're never far.
They glisten in the sky,
like my eyes when you show me that you listen, by all your blessings.

I'm grateful for what you've done thus far.
Tranquillity and peace,
and your direction,
is all I need, to proceed, in this life full of trouble and strife.

You are my love, you are my guide
You are my peace of mind.

THOSE MORNINGS

Watching Richard and Judy as you read the two papers I brought you.
How they brightened your day like the
''The Sun'' and ''The Mirror''
And the horse racing shortly after.

The smell of the orange you gave me half of
in the air like the love you shared, always equal, always fair.

I remember combing your hair, picking out the grey.
Never did I think there would ever be a day,
where I didn't get to hear all those things you used to say.

Remember how you always took my fear and pain away?

I still hear your footsteps,
your words of wisdom, I still feel your love.
Your voice, your commitments.

Your memories will never fade, my love for you will never sway. I see you in my dreams as
clear as day, always beg for you to stay.

When I saw you that day. I lay my head on your chest, cried like a baby as your soul slipped
away. Through thick apologies for not being around, I jumped as your soul flew away. I knew
you heard me.

I know you'll always hear me.

We may not have our garden anymore, but I still plant fruit and veg, plant roses, in memory of
you. As they bloom so do the things you taught me, everything you gave me. You will never
really go.

TO FORGIVE

To forgive you means in theory I have to forget the pain, the blame, the shame you put me through.

To accept that even though I explained the effect your actions had on me
you continued to do as you do.

No regard for the impact.

You spread your own truth and disregarded the facts
and through love or stupidity I took you back.

Took a chance on what clearing never was.
Heard your excuses and all your stories of all your wins but you never attempt to say sorry or right your sins.

I refuse to take your blame, for you knew what you were doing.
You knew what you were saying.
I refuse to continue to play your game.

Look in the mirror and answer yourself.
On judgement day, you tell them your excuses.
I've dealt with all those bruises.

Dealing with the impact of my choices, heard all those voices.
Forgiveness will not come from me.
I loved you but It meant nothing to you then and means nothing to you now.

A NEW BEGINNING

The flowers are beginning to bloom,
whilst the trees are changing their leaves back to green.

The skies are no longer gloomy.
Sometime-ish sunshine and smiling faces can be seen.
The birds are mating,
The bees are back.
Couples are summer dating.

Ice cream vans back in action.
Kids lining up for their treats.
Kids playing out in the not so safe streets.

The parks are full.
An indication of the beginning of a new season.

Just a reason,
to have get togethers, bbqs, and picnics
full of drink, love, sandwiches, and pick and mix.

Another season, another reason for a new beginning.

MY FAIRYTALE

When I played princess I put Grandma's tea cosies or towels on my head. Now my hair flows, I can flick it like my classmates. The classmates that strung me up on the wall and ripped my blue dungaree button because I was me.

I was a princess in a castle until the king changed. Jekyll and Hyde.

Sometimes despite my beautiful blessings, it's hard to feel somewhat elated. I Swam with the pretty mermaids and the ugly sharks until the Tsunami came.

Castle down. Picking up the pieces that remain//fractured and crumbled. Particles falling through my fingers, the dust flowing through the toxic air as it lingers.
Head count, couple special numbers down.
We loved them then and we love them now.
R.i.P—as we pour your favourite liquor on the ground//drowning the scary monsters and the ghosts//because we only do sweet angels here.

SHE STOOD TALL IN THE FACE OF ADVERSITY

She stood tall in the face of adversity.

Arrived on the wind rush leaving the sun, the sea, love, and kindness for the unknown, the cold not just from the frost but from its people.

But she stood tall.

She encouraged, she flourished, and she nourished.

She gave, she had a heart full of love, and she was brave.
She passed on not only wisdom and courage, knowledge and homemade recipes but she inspired a generation x 3.

I am inspired to be just like her.

To always love, to always give, to always pray, to sing and hum//on good and bad days.

She stood tall
She was her.

A PATHWAY TO BEAUTIFUL PEACE

I see a pathway of the brightest light.
Granted, there's so much scope, with endless rope but there's always an honest pathway to beautiful hope.

Air raids, modern slaves, any form of abuse and inequality
    we cannot not look away
including starvation/child emancipation/evil and dark temptation.

We can overcome any feeling of desperation.
With love and kindness, understanding and appreciation/for each other, we can fill the gaps and end our social segregation.
No more wars, children dying on floors and in desperate hospital wards.

Let's not succumb to what we cannot change, but walk together towards what we can.

Let's look towards a pathway to peace
an unknown, unwalked journey that's undoubtedly steep.

There's a way out even when the rivers are deep.
When you feel like you're drowning just keep treading, floating, keep your head above the water, find your inner saviour, and swim to the other side—to the pathway of peace,

Let's be that pathway to peace.

YOU ARE THE BEGINNING

I look down at you
in disbelief.

The greatest gift I have been given.

A new beginning.

A life
Half of me.

All my hopes and wishes came true, in you.

A new beginning.

Given all my losses, with you, I am truly winning

You are the truth.
The Purity that lays within you encourages my honesty, empathy and commitment.

You are my fulfilment.

You are the beginning.

BLACK PANTHER

Man of your work

Everyone saw it

Everyone felt it

Everyone heard it

Man of your word

Black panther

Worldwide movie

You all made history

Inspired little ones to just be

Regardless of colour or creed

You are a part of that, it's a part of your legacy

Your word was never overshadowed by money, fame nor greed

Now we all hope you are resting in peace

We hope you are flying high and feel free

Thank you for inspiring a generation

BUTTERFLY

Blue skies
The smell of freshly cut grass
a songbird's lullaby,
gives me butterflies.

Like them I wish I could fly.
Wings so pretty
spirit so free
demons cannot catch thee.

They glide so delicately.
They land where the heart desires,
smelling daisies before they are picked and trampled upon
just like the wings of the butterfly that lay broken upon the floor
the beautiful butterfly is no more.

DEAR TWITTER

I love the way you connect me with the world.
How I see the world in all of its glory,
hope and all of its stories.

Good, bad, wicked, and evil.
Pretty and beautiful.
Romantic and political.

Dear Twitter
You have the magic and mystery of a unicorn.
The power and destruction of a storm,
engaging users from night to dawn.
Making and breaking.

—such a platform

The ability to see from here to anywhere.
All over the world we're connected,
works of art, people—rejected and accepted
loved and hated
praised and slated

all in one day.

FLOWER

Pick me out, choose from the rest.
Smell me, caress me
make me feel like the best.
Water me, talk to me, pick out all my flaws and help me throw them away. Watch me bloom
with love//fill the room with beautiful colours.

That exotic aroma, fragrance of love in the air, igniting the passion.
Feel the spiritual aurora.

Perfect setting,
Two worlds colliding into one picture.
Cheese, wine.
This our time, we can flip the music back and rewind or
stay in this picture that we framed, and freeze.
Just you and I, everyone else can leave.

Take a moment and listen to me breathe.

Place your hand on my heart, promise to never make it bleed.
Place the ring upon my finger and promise to never leave.
Pick up my veil, kiss my lips after we say til death do us part and just before you take me by the
waist and we have our first dance. And just after

we set off, to create memories as if it was our last chance.

FORGIVE ME FOR WAS I ANGRY

Forgive me for I was angry for the dreams of fairytales and unicorns I once had, that was not to be.

Images of serenity and peace that was snatched from me/like sweets from a kid/in the street/never to return.

—albeit for now

Until the tide returns and the water re-emerges leaving behind
only the shoreline. The tell-tell sign of the history that lay between these waters and the land.

Water slapping against the rocks, as history repeats itself.

The waves revisiting over and over,
knocking me
to the seabed
until I learned to swim, to surf, even to float, to glide through the tide.

I now swim with the dolphins, the mermaids and the sharks and I make it back to shore every single time.

YOUR INNER BEAUTY

Hey there!

You see that doubt that you have? it's normal but
let it go.
The world is beautiful, let your insecurities go.

You have so much to give, let it show.
You are amazing, your talents and the way you think
let your inner beauty glow.

Do not compromise your beliefs, do not be selfish but
anything that you do not want to do, tell them 'no.'
Never do something that will make you live with regrets
you only get one life, make it the best.

Learn new knowledge and wisdom and let that digest.
Travel the world,
explore in its entirety,
in this life there are only a few guarantees…
tax and death…so love, live and laugh
until your last breath.
Keep trying until you have nothing left.

In your darkest hour
like a bird with mended wings,
analyse when you are ready, take off and rise.

There will be sadness and you will cry//but there will also be laughter and joy.

Don't let anyone ever let you doubt yourself,

whether you are loud or coy.

As long as you care and are selfless it's okay.

Be your best and you will flourish,

always use your inner strength and have courage.

And all those scars you have, they are a part of who you are,

it's what makes you that shining star//

don't be afraid to show them, they are your stripes

they will show how you've overcome all your strikes.

I assure you, willpower, love, kindness and loyalty is what gets real 'likes.'

Those little moments of happiness, embrace it.

Your wishes and dreams go and chase it.

Stay healthy and be the best you can be,

as I promise you, ain't nothing better than your inner beauty!

GIANTS

We stand tall like giants but really we feel like
we're ants marching in the ground.
Stamping us out while we
march without sound -but- the silence is so loud.

We're an army.
They can't break our colony.
Take a bow—we'll take a knee.
We'll stand until we're free
She sat so we could speak.
Black that is me.

GRANDMA

Our sweet caring Grandma
We want to thank you for being you
We want to thank you for your everlasting love
Your words of courage and wisdom
Your endless kindness and your unconditional hugs

We want to thank you for all the great Christmas's you made
And all our birthday cakes that you baked
Those long days and nights in the kitchen making delicious food that we all ate
I will always remember our shopping trips to Tesco's and Wrigleys where you bought me a toy
every week because you couldn't say no
The love you and Grandad instilled in us will always show
And we will pass it down to our kids as they grow
Just like your special recipes
Including your own herbal remedies
And your juice

We will never forget you
Our memories of you will never fade
You will live on in every way
In all that we say and every time we pray
We are a part of you, and you a part of us and you will never truly die
As you will live on

In the music we hear
In the stars in the sky
In the food that we eat
In our dancing feet
In the perfume that we wear
Through the hope in the air
In the love that we share
You will never die as you will live on

I SEE YOU BLOWING IN THE WIND

I see you blowing in the wind //losing your leaves in the cold// glowing in the sun// regaining life//It never gets old// watching the way you move//side to side//so mysterious.

You see it all//everything and everyone that passes and everything that rises and falls.
You stand so tall even though you're surrounded by walls.
Your light always shines//ever so green//and even when your green goes brown//you still stand tall—never falling down.

Although you may shake//your elegance and beauty is only lost through man-made and weathered breaks.

The way you give life
with each breath//I take//
I feel you//need you//my oxygen.

The way they use you,
from the palm oil to the paper//they mistreat you.
I adore you//from the finest leaf//to the tallest branch
you are shelter and warmth//and where the apples and pears grow.

Where the beauty and nature of the beast shows.
Where the birds and the bees go.
You are where hope grows.

Memories of swinging and climbing//jumping and hiding.
Picking conkers and finding//ladybirds, squirrels, and nests.
Watching the chicks hatch//and take their first breath.
Magical moments all found because of you.
So tall and so elegant//giving life.

LET'S READ TOGETHER

Open me like a book and turn my pages

Smell my sweet scent reminiscent of the flowers
   you bought me.

Read my intellect,
     between the sheets—intuition.

This book is full of mystery—we're on a two-way mission. Suspense-the thrill-and
Romanticism.

Lights out—the candles are lit.

Absorbing the words that flow from the sheets to the lips
   reading in unison like dancing with your hands on my hips

We re-read and examine the cover
  —explore the scripts
as the temperature flips.

Let's let the story exercise our imagination
explore and be left in utter fascination.

Let's rewrite and read our history.

Strip me of insecurities and feed me with strawberry flavoured inspiration.

Look at my body of work
　　whilst being intrigued and full of sweet admiration.
Feed me with guided aspiration.

We're dripping words of knowledge
　　Knowledge is our power
the power is in the book

This book has it all—
　　Catch me at the climax
—it's left me on a high
　　I don't want to fall

Grace me with your wisdom and your flows of passion
　　　　I don't want this to end
let's depart in a timely fashion

Don't leave my heart in scars and me, the colour ashen

let us read and rewrite our book full of love, freedom and passion

I'M FROM THAT COUNCIL ESTATE

I'm from that council estate.
That leave some of us in fragile states.
It seems we're trapped like being behind those sturdy gates.

Stuck in the hood and where only some get breaks.

From a hood where, I watch,
kids play paper, scissors, and rock
and the felons plot
while the shotters shot.
The shooters shoot
the feds sit and watch.

All the mums praying it stops.
Another mother crying for a dead son,
another life—flops.
Another tear, oh dear, how they drip drop
where I'm from, on this block.

Where the council make promises but never follow through,
where we're left to exist
in the damp and the mould and the rot
with the rats and the roaches
in the dark and the cold
and everyone knows but if they turn a blind eye, then no one knows.

They say there's no stigma but when you give out your address they turn up their nose.

They talk of gangs but you have these kids trapped in these blocks from young, no garden just the estate,
out like an easy target—alternative-no play.
Now they're teenagers, you're talking about hoodies and gangs
this is where these boys hang.

Above all, being in these estates could mean getting flocked,
kids getting bullied and mocked.

Coming home's a hazard,
on the balcony watching my boy make it back from school through the gangs and guns, knives and drugs.
I tell him son, mind your your phone you might get mugged,
never take anything from anyone son, you might get drugged.
Mind your manners with the police, they kill innocent people like you and I, no mercy, no justice and definitely no peace.
Careful son, this world isn't an eye for an eye
It's just you, God, and I.

HOPE HAS TWO BEAUTIFUL DAUGHTERS; THEIR NAMES ARE ANGER AND COURAGE.

When we cut we bleed the same but we have separate hearts
represented by the many differences that push us apart
Some of our differences may leave us with scars
issues of self-consciousness
issues of unfairness
issues of unlawfulness

We could be pushed backwards and we could be failed because of all the injustice

Equality and learning from past history is imperative, it's all informative

We need to eradicate injustice

We need to stop practicing racism, sexism and all the other negative -isms
Instead love and promote our unique individualism
the aim is that the future generation will have a better and clearer vision
and be free from this mental prison
and the future will be free from all the torture of the injustices of our socialism

We could be angry at the anger and hate that we see,
let it consume us and be unhappy
we can turn a blind eye and be a part of hypocrisy
Or we can,
be hopeful like St Augustine's
Hope.
Hope has two beautiful daughters;
Anger and Courage.

Anger at the way things are and Courage to see that they do not remain as they are

there can be change, we can be the change

Our wonderful differences—we need to embrace and encourage,

grow and nourish,

water and let it flourish,

like the birds, clip their wings and let them fly

the world is our oyster, we can reach the sky

let go of all our inhibitions

reach our full potential and fulfil our dreams and ambitions

We need positivity

stronger connections within the community

help for our families

understanding and unity

let's avoid mutiny

We need equality

and learning from past history is imperative, it's all informative.

We need to stop practicing racism, sexism and all the other negative -isms

Instead love and promote our unique individualism.

We should,

be hopeful that the future generation will have a better and clearer vision

that they will be free from this mental torture, social prison

of all the injustices of our socialism.

Grant us the serenity to accept the things we cannot change, the courage to change the things we

can

and the wisdom to know the difference.

Let us be the change, let us be the difference

LOVE THAT WE FOUND

I'm not sure if it was those late night McDonald's drive thru's
    the Big Macs...
while I twiddled my hair and picked the sauce off your lap.

Or those soppy love films that we hugged, got close, and I cried to.
  But I am committed to our love and the energy that shines through you.

The way that you hold me,

      it's like a metaphor for the telephone—
close to your lips/your hold is so strong/tight grip
        your fingers pressing all the right buttons.
   Talking—so only I can hear,
Two-way connection.
    Whispers of sweet nothings—ear to ear.
        I don't want to disconnect—and don't you dare.

I want to stay in orbit—in this love—going around and around.
      Raise your glasses—here's to love that was nearly lost but found.
Our own little love revolution.
      You are my equal, my solution, our own little love evolution.

YOU ARE ESSENTIAL AND YOU KNOW IT!

Broken or unbroken, you are essential.

Perfect life's or external and internal fights/it's our life—we all live, love, cry and laugh—

It's not Black or white.

Like the oxygen that I breathe you energise me, like the air that I feel on any day, you elevate me,

Empower me

The way that you are unique to each and everyone/you're special and you know it!

The way you have the ability to light up a room, on the greatest and even on the hardest days.

The way you portray yourself through everyone in small, big and all different ways.

You put a smile on all our faces,
You get us out of all the darkest and narrowest places.

You are always there on our best days
and we most definitely need you on our worst days.

Without you I do not know where we'd be.

Please do not ever leave, keep surrounding us with your pure beauty/glorious memories /with your everlasting touch of what came before and what will most definitely live on.

You Love,

my love,

could never be too much, you are essential.

Love is essential.

YOUR LOSS IS MY LOSS AND I CRY TOO

I waited all my life for you
to look after you, guide and nurture you.

To affectionately tease you and then to eventually send you to the shop once you were old
enough, like we all were sent on errands that we didn't want to do.

But that wasn't to be.

For your perfection didn't see the sweet light of day.
15 years of hope just slipped away.

The only thing we ever shared was our mother's womb.

The excitement, the hopes and dreams
faded in a painful but calm instant.

Your soul and body returned as quickly as it nearly came.
Life on the floor, bloodstained.

To walk away, without you
never officially named, loss that could never be explained,
but you are my brother, and I felt your loss, I too, felt that pain.

THIS FEELS LIKE A MOMENT

Our eyes meet.
It's like we've met before—familiarity,

yet we're strangers in passing
and now we're asking...what is your name?

I am asking about one's day
not knowing what might be the wrong or right things to say.

I'm looking into your eyes and I'm feeling some type of way. I have funny feelings in my belly,
I am shaking and my legs are feeling like jelly.

Will you get to strip me? Will I get to my bare soul? All your fears and troubles will you share
them with me and let them go?

Will we both undeniably show, that we are both in it for the long game?
Maybe one day we may even get our picture in a perfect frame.

Will you stand tall on those nights you want to cower? Will you strip me of my insecurities and
shower me with love even when I'm easy to hate?

First you have to look past these brown eyes and into a half broken heart that in coalition
sometimes cries.

Maybe, forgive me for my sins, celebrate my wins and comfort my losses,

whilst I take you for everything you are and everything you stand for.

Elevate you and to help you to achieve and believe, in your power.

This feels like a moment.
Could this be a moment that we remember for a lifetime?

GUILTY

I stood before the Judge. Dressed as smart as I could. Black blazer, a prestigious white shirt. He asked, "how do you plead?"

I looked at my 6 inch red bottom heels, wishing I was Dorothy, wishing I could go back to a place I could call home. I looked up, took a deep breath and I said, ''Guilty your Honour.

I am guilty as I stand before you here today//of giving my all, my very best and still failing at the notion that it was enough.

I stand here, guilty, with a heart full of love that was broken over and over—it now knows not how to love without building barriers and walls that one cannot knock down.

Although they try—with giant hammers and sledges and even noisy bulldozers—the wall does not break.

I am guilty of having the knowledge that I wished I once had. I wallow and I swim in it. It sometimes feels like I am drowning in it.

Then I reach for the float //the life jacket// that the sexy dark-haired Lifeguard threw to me and at once I'm back on dry land. Fighting for air, fighting for life. Everyone is looking with opinions and concerned stares. As the sun beams, opinions and egos flare.

I am guilty your Honour of overthinking, overworking, and not appreciating the little things, always looking for the bigger things.

Always looking for the next move because stopping means being still.

At night is when it's at its worst.

I should be asleep and while my body is still my mind is racing but there is no end and there is not a winner.

Your Honour, I am guilty of, failing to see the beauty that has already been planted and flowered and continues to be watered. I am guilty your Honour."

"As you have plead guilty in the court of law, I hereby sentence you to life

of abundance of self love and understanding, patience and kindness to yourself and others.

Dedication to your cause//and cover from all that's not meant to be yours.

To see the sunrise and sunset, to see it, believe it and to be it....take her down."

DIAMOND

Dig her out of the dirt with my bare hands,
clean her up and let her shine.

Little rough around edges, jagged and sharp
but she twinkles
when she shines.

Place her in your loving heart,
hold her in palm, in your tight grasp.

Priceless yet so expensive.
Pure and so sought after.

Hold her in your hands and never let her go.
Precious and delicate, feed and nourish her soul and let her know, so

she will shine bright, even when it rains
and pours, she will know that her sweet sparkle is forever yours.

ALWAYS EMPOWERED

You look at me as I look at you,
those sweet brown eyes, once full of hope and admiration now full of concern.

My eyes full of love, hope, and power
wide eyes now seem
blank.
What are you thinking? Are you thinking?

My once strong body now filled with medicine and worry.
As it slowly takes over, remember who I was and who I am.

Know that I am still here and that I still am,
everything I was. Do not pity me. I am still me. I am still everything I was.

I embraced the beautiful, the pure, the evil, the sacred.
Even with all the struggles, our love and memories we hold dear will always make it.

When emotions of sadness take over, remember the memories of yesterday and all precious
ones yet to be made.

Hold me by the hand, feel the power and be empowered and together we'll always stand.

Whether physically or in memory, the power of our love will always be,
a part of you and a part of me.

Integrity, confidence, understanding and resilience is what we need.

Peace and unity is what we'll forever stand for.

Empowered is what we'll always be.

EMPTY CHAIR

I am empty as is, your favourite chair.

Where you used to eat, where you used to do your hair,
where you would pray, show love, and where you would care.

Where you gave anything and everything and where you have left something—more than
materials and time but knowledge and wisdom and your empty chair.

The dark days, when the wind sways, I wish you would cradle me, instead I sit in your empty
chair, its arms never replacing yours, though it tries.
It no longer feels your fear and you are no longer there. All that is left is the hurt in my chest
and the awful smell of death. The feeling of guilt, knowing I should have done more, listened to
your stories of your own personal war.
Our culture of history, family genealogy.
Instead I stare at your empty chair.

It sits alone in its own deserted space. It will never get to hold you and feel your embrace, one
last time but I can and always will see your beautiful face in your empty chair. Bitter air on my
face, I am forever in awe of you have done and taught us and that will live on, along with your
empty chair.

NOTES ON PREVIOUS PUBLICATIONS

Grandma and Grandad

Protests

Chambers-Ghost Heart Literary Journal- Scotland Sep 2020

Unite

Fly on the wall magazine- Manchester- September 2020

Black

Dying to bloom

Visions of possibilities

Melbourne culture centre-Australia -October 2020

Yesterday

Morepork Press-New Zealand-September 2020

Black panther

Daily Drunk Mag -USA-September 2020

One heart

You

Saccharine-England-October 2020

And she lives on

Ice floe poetry -USA- November 2020

My Destiny-

Alien Buddha Press- USA October 2020

Misery loves company

Hope

Travelling In Mind-

I Am POET (WAVE 5)-March 2021

I am more than my hair

I will wear my crown

Harpy Hybrid-March 2021

Lockdown (Covid issue)

Gemini- April /May -2021

Competitions

Let's Read Together

Halton library - first prize - March 2021

Pathway to Beautiful Peace

Waltham Forest writes competition - third prize - September 2021